T0126436

Secrets in the Sand

Secrets in the Sand

———

The Young Women of Ciudad Juárez

A Bilingual Volume

Poems by Marjorie Agosín

Translated and with a critical introduction by
Celeste Kostopulos-Cooperman

White Pine Press • Buffalo, New York

Publication of this book was made possible by support from the Judith
Stronach Fund of the Vanguard Public Foundation, by public funds from the
New York State Council on the Arts, a State Agency, and by a grant from the
National Endowment for the Arts, which believes that a great nation deserves
great art.

NATIONAL
ENDOWMENT
FOR THE ARTS

Printed and bound in the United States of America.

First Edition

Cover image: "The Border" by Lydia Martin. Oil on linen, 18" x 24".

ISBN 1-893996-47-6
13-digit ISBN: 978-1-893996-47-2

Library of Congress Control Number: 2005934741

Published by
White Pine Press
P.O. Box 236
Buffalo, New York 14201
www.whitepine.org

In memory of Judith Stronach
and with gratitude for believing in this book.
M.A. & C.K.C.

To the families left behind. . .

Acknowledgments

On a clear September morning four years ago Judith Strolnick called me unexpectedly to tell me that she admired my work in human rights. Then she asked me about my future projects. I told her that I was thinking about creating a volume of poems about the young women of Juárez who reminded me so much of the disappeared women of my own country. Judith quickly urged me to write the book and said that she would fund it.

Time passed and I wrote about Juárez, all the while wanting to become better acquainted with the magical voice that called me one day from California. Judith died tragically but her spirit lives in these verses, in her devotion to human rights and to poetry. It is to her living memory that I wish to dedicate this book.

—Marjorie Agosín

A translator's vision is always enhanced by the readings of others who bring their own cultural insights to the words on the written page. I would like to thank colleagues and friends who have inspired me to search for a language that is powerful yet seamless in its transition from Spanish to English. To Marjorie Agosín for generously inviting me to join her in this important project, to Mark Schafer for his time and critical commentary and to the editors of White Pine who continue to support art that is committed to the search for truth and justice. Finally, a project of this magnitude could not have been possible without the love of my husband and children who have always been my primary source of hope and encouragement.

—Celeste Kostopulos-Cooperman

Table of Contents

Poems by Guadalupe Morfín

PREFACE

—

Secrets in the Sand:
The Young Women of Juárez

Celeste Kostopulos-Cooperman

GROWING OVER A SMALL piece of earth in the shadows of the peaks of Cuernos de la Luna is a colorful cluster of fragile flowers that seems to cast a watchful eye over the otherwise abandoned site. The Virgin of Guadalupe's presence hovers in this sacred place, protecting the spirits of the dead.

In this high desert region where few plants grow and snakes and deadly spiders live among the thorny bushes, the remains of another murdered woman were found in December of 2003. Her name was Neyra Azucena Cervantes. Given the remoteness of the place, it's difficult to imagine how the ruthless murderer who abandoned her here after commiting his heinous crime forcibly dragged this young student from Chihuahua up the mountain.

At the time of this writing, the family of Neyra is still not convinced that the bones found here are those of their daughter, even though pieces of clothing belonging to the young woman were recovered at the site. There can be no consolation for the family of this girl. Nor can there be any hope for the families of the countless other disappeared women who were no doubt murdered by the unknown killers who still freely roam the streets. In the state of Chihuahua, as Lourdes Portillo poignantly observes in her documentary film, *Señorita Extraviada*, "the desert is filled with secrets."

In a country whose "machista" culture often accuses women of provoking their abusers, predators are unafraid of a system of justice that for the past decade has failed to protect the lives of its most vulnerable citizens. Their murders undetected by police surveillance patrols, the remains of these young women continue to be found scattered on the parched desert sand, in vacant city lots, and in roadside ditches raped, strangled and mutilated beyond recognition. In some cases the desert sun has scorched their beautiful tan skin or their bones have been picked clean by wild animals. Who is killing these beautiful, innocent victims, robbing them of their youth and of the possibility to live out their dreams?

Ciudad Juárez, the largest city in the state of Chihuahua, is a prominent manufacturing municipality with approximately 2.1 million residents. Once the capital of the Mexican government

(1865), it was named after Benito Juárez who led resistance forces against the French occupation in the mid-nineteenth century. It has been the gateway between North and South for more than three centuries, and in the early 1990s it epitomized the promises of the North American Free Trade Agreement (NAFTA), which has created jobs for more than 1.2 million Mexicans, approximately 250,000 in Juárez alone.

Waves of migrants flood the city's streets, searching for employment in an industry that has reached capacity and can no longer accommodate the numbers of individuals who left behind miserable conditions in search of better lives. Many of them are "campesinos," poor farmers who have come from as far as Oaxaca, Veracruz and Durango. Thousands are women and girls who have worked only in domestic settings. Living conditions for the large majority of the migrants are wretched. Neighborhoods of sheet metal and cardboard dwellings and single-room concrete cubicles coexist in an urban district fringed by sprawling industrial parks. The city has grown beyond its means and its infrastructure is incapable of handling the large numbers of migrants. It cannot afford to house, educate or adequately serve its inhabitants. Thousands of residents have no running water or electricity and about 1,100 miles of city roads are unpaved. Although foreign investment has brought prosperity to the region, creating opportunities where none previously existed, globalization has exacerbated the conditions that contribute to instability, particularly in the border towns, and has undeniably created a "new" market for undesirable elements that feed off the vulnerability of the urban poor living on the margin.

Employing thousands of young men and women who come from the most impoverished regions of Mexico, the assembly plants, or *maquilas* have given rise to what many consider to be a modern cultural revolution. Approximately sixty percent of the workers are female and their average weekly salary is fifty-five dollars. Some speculate that the addition of women and young girls to the labor force, and their increasing access to financial and social independence, has aggravated traditional "machista" elements in the region, thus spawning even more violence against females. According to Guadalupe Ramirez, the director of a small organization that tracks the cases of disappeared women and girls, "The men don't respect women who leave the house to work. They think they can assault them, that they can insult them, that they can walk by and touch them."[1]

Since the early 1990s, Juárez has earned the distinction of having among the highest homicide rates in all of Mexico. However, the killings are no longer confined to drug feuds and gang fights, and men are not the sole victims of the violence. The vacant lots and stretches of desert that line the border have become dumping grounds for the bodies of large numbers of women and girls, whose bones and clothing are tossed like garbage in roadside ditches and open tracts of abandoned land.

Pink crosses painted on the telephone poles that rise from the dry earth serve as monuments to the dead. They are constant reminders of the silenced victims whose brutal deaths demand that justice be served. They also underscore the need for serious measures to be taken to provide for the safety and protection of the women and girls living in the city who are most vulnerable to the predators that continue to threaten their lives yet escape punishment from local, state and federal authorities.

Some strongly suspect that the murderers freely cross the border from Texas or New Mexico, and that they live and work in neighboring U.S. cities and towns. It's striking to observe that the city of El Paso, just across the Rio Grande from Ciudad Juárez, has been recognized as the fourth safest city in the United States.

Although local officials have documented approximately 340 murders of women in the region, international human rights organizations estimate that far more have been killed. Amnesty International estimates more than 370 killings of women in Ciudad Juárez and Chihuahua. The files of Special Prosecutor

María López Urbina confirm 349 cases of female homicides. But in Juárez, facts are sketchy, evidence is falsified and truth is ignored. Families of the disappeared and murdered young women are living an endless nightmare. Citizens live in fear, with no confidence in the police or in the state, federal and local authorities, who have failed them at every turn. The city is under a state of siege, where innocents are incarcerated and fathers demanding justice have been threatened and tortured.

Chihuahua is not a police state, but the terror felt by a large portion of its citizenry is the same. Octavio Paz, poet, Nobel Prize Laureate and visionary, observed many years ago that terror and repression, like propaganda and totalitarian political action, obey the same system. Propaganda distributes incomplete truths that become organized and transformed into political theories and absolute truths for the masses. Persecution, on the other hand, begins in certain isolated groups until it gradually affects everyone. At first, some of the people indifferently observe the extermination of certain social groups or contribute to their persecution, exacerbating internal hatreds. Eventually and tragically, however, all become accomplices to the terror and the guilt which pervade the whole of the affected society.[2]

After more than a decade of brutal slayings, abductions, misinformation, negligence and obstruction of justice, the families of the victims are, tragically, no closer to the truth. Law enforcement has failed miserably to identify the perpetrators of these crimes against humanity, and there have been few convictions, among them that of Abdel Latif Sharif, an Egyptian-born engineer who has remained in custody since his most recent appeal. In July of 1998 the National Human Rights Commission (CNDH) concluded that the judicial, state and municipal authorities were guilty of negligence and dereliction of duty.[3] There is general unrest because the crimes continue, and the fear that stalks the streets of Juárez is palpable. There is no way of getting rid of it because too many citizens have been touched by it personally and no longer feel themselves immune to the nightmares that relentlessly remind them of the missing.

In her film, Lourdes Portillo remarks that, "More attention is paid to economic development plans than to human beings." Francisco Barrio, Mexican President Vicente Fox's anti-corruption czar, expressed a rather matter-of-fact attitude toward the femicides, once stating in an interview that "the murder rate in Juárez is not abnormal for a city of its size."

According to Esther Chávez Cano a pioneer in the Juárez Women's Movement and founder in 1998 of Casa Amiga, a rape and abuse crisis center, the killings continue and the authorities and *maquila* owners have done very little to change the conditions which cause them. Policies at the plants continue to endanger their employees. The most outrageous is the rule that turns workers away if they are as little as three minutes late. Workers begin and end their late night shifts with no police or security patrols to protect them.[4] To make matters worse, the young women who have been brutally murdered suffer a second death when a negligent press that accuses them of being drug addicts and prostitutes slanders their reputations.

Many politicians and business leaders have seemed more concerned with image and marketing than with the most basic of human rights. Victor Valencia, the speaker for the Chihuahua State Legislature, has publicly denounced the popular band, "Los Tigres del Norte," for promoting their song about the murdered women of Ciudad Juárez. According to Valencia, the ballad "Las mujeres de Juárez" sullies the state's reputation and tarnishes the image of the city. It is also harmful when Chávez Cano and other NGOs are discredited by the Mexican press when they have been among the first to recognize, document and denounce the gender-based violence which prevents the victims from fulfilling their "civil, political, economic, social and cultural rights."[5] Threats against human rights defenders and organizations and divisiveness among groups trying to help the families also stand as major stumbling blocks to the search for truth and justice.

Newspapers such as *El Diario*, claim that women's groups have exaggerated the situation and that Juárez has an "image problem" more than a crime problem. Several business leaders have also denied that the growth of the *maquila* industry has had anything to do with the series of killings of women and girls in the region. A common perception still seems to be that of Carlos Rosetti who, in the summer of 2000 as the spokesman for Mexico's National Maquiladora Industry Council, denied complicity of the industry in the murders. "We don't feel guilty about offering people jobs. You can't fault the industry at all. It has nothing to do with the killings."[6]

Created in 1965, the *maquiladoras* form part of a special commercial zone where foreign companies import parts "duty-free" and export finished products at favorable tax and labor rates. Exports from the industry are worth more than ten billion dollars a year. These assembly plants were built for profit, despite the claims of many that boast of their role in strengthening the Mexican economy. The availability of cheap labor and the lack of independent unions make it nearly impossible for employees to defend themselves against an industry that demonstrates little concern for the safety of its workers once they have left company grounds. Some companies continue to exploit illegal child labor and scarcely make an effort to verify the documents of birth that are in their files.

Civic groups not only continue to pressure state and federal authorities to accept responsibility for the crimes but they also continue to capture worldwide attention by attracting the intervention of organizations within the United Nations and the Inter-American Commission of Human Rights. However, as Chávez Cano and others have observed, politics seems to override concern for the victims and their families. When a girl is reported missing there is still no immediate criminal investigation and failure of the justice system to do its job causes deep distrust of authority. Important information is frequently ignored and officials have been offensive to families and have not heeded what could have been life saving data.

The Mexican justice system is faced with a daunting challenge.

In Ciudad Juárez and Chihuahua women and young girls continue to disappear and no one can seem to put a stop to the indiscriminate nature of the violence. In response to the growing domestic and international concern with the killings, in October 2003 and January 2004, President Vicente Fox appointed María Guadalupe Morfín Otero as the special federal commissioner on violence against women and María López Urbina as the special federal prosecutor to investigate the murders of women in Ciudad Juárez. In their first six months in office, both women recognized the importance of responding rapidly and efficiently to investigate new cases that come to the attention of authorities. They also strongly criticized state and local institutions for gross negligence in handling evidence and for their complicity in failing to protect the murdered women and the families that are left behind.

Local legislators, labor-union leaders and students among others have formed organizations such as the Coalition on Violence Against Women and Families on the Border, Friends of the Women of Juárez, and the Mexico Solidarity Network to investigate the murders and search for ways to prevent these horrific crimes. Efforts to offer support and justice to the families of the disappeared and murdered women have extended beyond the Rio Grande and have become matters of international attention. Binational groups continue to form along the border and elsewhere insisting that the Juárez deaths are not just a Mexican concern and most certainly not just a women's issue. The escalating pattern of violence against women and young girls extends beyond the "ordinary domain of domestic violence." The vast majority of the victims are not women living in abusive relationships. There is much to accomplish and it will be through the collective efforts of people within the Mexican and international communities that the human rights of all will be protected and that the guilty will be found. The implementation of Guadalupe Morfín's "Forty Point Plan" and its recommendations to prevent violence against women must be supported so that the causes of the abuse will be eliminated from the social fabric of a society whose most vulnerable citizens have been severely threatened and traumatized.[7]

Like the mothers of the Plaza de Mayo and the Chilean *arpilleristas* the women of Ciudad Juárez and Chihuahua have refused to acquiesce and remain silent. By sharing their grief and defying the criminals who roam the city streets with impunity, they comfort one another and strengthen their resolve to face the terror that has destroyed their lives. Bearing photographs of their beloved daughters they accompany each other and struggle to demand justice from authorities who have done little to earn their respect and trust. Some cling to the desperate hope that their children will someday return. Others live daily with the knowledge that their girls were brutally attacked and murdered. The pain in their hearts and the fortitude of their spirit are testaments to their solidarity and courage to confront the challenges that lie ahead.

In this volume of poetry dedicated to the women of Juárez, Marjorie Agosín, through words and unsettling images, invites her readers to feel and witness the reality that the grieving families of the disappeared and murdered young women and girls face every day of their lives. Surrounded by the spirits of the living-dead, she probes beneath the surface and searches for clues that lie buried in the desert sands. She demands accountability and truth where others have fallen into silence. As a poet and human rights activist, Agosín is familiar with subjects that are disturbing in their content and provocative in their nature. The granddaughter of Russian and Viennese Jews who settled in South America after fleeing the hatred and racism of early twentieth century Europe, she has dedicated her life to the search for justice and human dignity. In an earlier volume of poetry she beautifully observes that, "When human rights are violated so is the sacredness of our world. . . Memory, courage and the right to remember and give voice are also human rights."[8]

The poems that fill the pages of this volume remind us all that we must not remain silent bystanders while the innocent young women and girls of Juárez and Chihuahua are being deprived of their right to live and dream. Concerned citizen action and binational support of the families of the disappeared and murdered must be maintained to keep pressure on federal, state and local authorities, as well as on the *maquila* industry. It is the responsibility of all civilized humanity to put an end to the nightmare that has deprived the young people of Ciudad Juárez and Chihuahua of laughter and hope. The world cannot afford to ignore these crimes against humanity that continue to destroy so many lives. The rights to life, physical integrity, liberty and personal safety must be protected and ensured whenever and wherever they are threatened.[9]

—Celeste Kostopulos-Cooperman
Suffolk University
Boston, MA, 2005

[1] "Nightmare in the City of Dreams," Molly E, Moore, www.washingtonpost.com., p. 4.

[2] Octavio Paz, *El laberinto de la soledad,* del capítulo, *Los hijos de la Malinche,* p. 62.

[3] See Irene Khan's report entitled "Intolerable killings: 10 years of abductions and murder of women in Ciudad Juárez and Chihuahua.,"Amnesty International, September 2003. p. 17 .

[4] Some companies claim to have improved security by encouraging their employees to attend safety sessions and by providing better transportation to and from the plants.

[5] Irene Khan, Report by the Secretary General of Amnesty International, September 2003, p. 24.

[6] "Nightmare in the City of Dreams," Molly E, Moore,www.washigtonpost.com., p. 7.

[7] *Informe de gestión.* Comisión para Prevenir y Erradicar la Violencia contra ls Mujeres de Ciudad Juárez, noviembre 2003-abril 2004, Secretaría de Gobernación.

[8] Marjorie Agosín, *An Absence of Shadows,* Preface, New York:White Pine Press, 1998.

[9] Rights contained in the American Convention on Human Rights and the International Covenant on Civil and Political Rights.

Secrets in the Sand

No había en aquellos sitiales
Ni plantas ni rocas.
Sólo la muerte desnuda y pérfida.
En aquellos páramos donde las encontraron
Había ciertos ecos llamados vacíos.

De sus muertes tan
Sólo la muerte
Espectacular vacío
Ausencia ahuecada
Silencios pérfidos
De sus muertes tan
Sólo interrogantes,
Rezos.

No plants or rocks
Were in those places
Only naked and perfidious death.
On the plains where they found them
There were certain empty echoes.

All we know about them
Is their death
Spectacular emptiness
Hollowed out absence
Perfidious silence.
About their deaths
Only questions,
Prayers.

Huerfanía

Ante la añoranza
Era el secreto recinto del silencio
Huía de las voces ajenas
Elegí la huerfanía
El contorno de todo lo sumergido
Busqué la voz en
Lo que no se oye.

Orphanhood

Before the longing
Was the secret zone of silence
Fleeing from foreign voices.
I chose orphanhood
I searched for the voice in
What cannot be heard.

Y la noche era como un precipicio
Y la noche era un sonido ahuecado,
Más allá de todos los sonidos y todos los silencios
Era la noche en Ciudad Juárez y las muertas de Juárez
Protegían a las vivas
Y la noche no parecía ser una noche en la frontera
Parecía más que nada al sopor del infierno mudo
A las llamas que se transforman en cuchillos.

La noche en Juárez era un espejo perverso
Donde el suspiro de la muerte posaba sobre la arena
sus cuencas y sus trofeos.

Y la noche en esa ciudad de Juárez no tenía ni principio ni fin
Tan solo el miedo
Tan solo la muerte.

And the night was a precipice,
And the night was a hollow sound,
Beyond all depths and silences.
It was night in the city of Juárez and the dead women of Juárez
Protected the living ones.
It didn't seem like a typical night at the border.
It seemed more like the drowsiness of a mute inferno
And flames transforming into knives.

Night in Juárez was a perverse mirror
Where death breathed its hollow
Trophies over the sand.

And night in the city of Juárez didn't have a beginning or an end
Just fear
Just death.

Entre las nubes que apaciguan las tormentas
Yo las veo
Son las mujeres de Juárez
Girando entre las sombras.

Mientras los hombres de la guerra
Desfilaban con sus tanques y sus cuchillos
Yo quería creer en
la posibilidad
de amar.

Among the clouds that soothe the storms
I see them
The dead women of Juárez
Twirling among the shadows.

While men of war
Paraded with their tanks and knives
I wanted to believe in
The possibility of
Loving.

Con los corazones tristes,
Como las amapolas cautivas
Otra vez ellas aguardan y aguardan
Llegan a la otra orilla
Algunas llegan
Algunas regresan.
Otras se encuentran como amapolas
Muertas en los desiertos
Algunas ya nadie recuerda
Algunas como amapolas rotas a las orillas
De todos los caminos.

With sorrowful hearts
Like captive poppies
They wait and wait again
They reach the other border
Some arrive
And some return.
Others are found like poppies
Dead in the desert
No longer remembered
Like the wilted poppies
At the edge of the roads.

Siempre al borde
Al borde de un camino
Al borde de la historia
Cortadas entre los bordes
Las mujeres de ciudad
Juárez
Al borde de la muerte
A las orillas del miedo
Pueblan a una ciudad amordazada
Al borde de la sombra
Al borde del tiempo
Una voz sin cuerpo
Nadie.

Always at the edge
At the edge of the road
At the edge of history
Severed between the borders
The young women of
Juárez
At the edge of death
At the shore of fear
Populate a gagged city
At the shadow's edge
At the edge of time
A disembodied voice
No body.

Y de pronto la ciudad se convirtió en una sola luz en una sola mirada en una sola historia. Las voces eran rugidos, murmullos, como un terciopelo desgarrado, y eran voces claras como los espejos del agua y eran voces que no dejaban de preguntar y susurrar y llamaban en el idioma del amor y llamaban en el idioma de la memoria.

Suddenly the city was transformed into one light, one gaze, one history. The voices were bellows and murmurs, like torn velvet. They were clear, like water mirrors. They were voices that didn't stop inquiring and whispering. They called in the language of love, in the language of memory.

Y ella cruzaba fronteras
Avanzaba
Giraba
Era osada en sus ires
Y venires
Llevaba cántaros de agua
Esperanza del color de agua.

Ella cruzaba fronteras,
Y en todas ellas,
La detenían,
La acusaban,
La revisaban
Como si fuera un ave malhechora.
Insaciable,
Determinada,
Feliz,
Ella cruzaba fronteras
Su cuerpo era un umbral
Donde el norte y el sur
Eran palabras claras
Para lavar la mirada
El corazón
Pulir las grietas.

She crossed borders
She approached,
Turned and
Was daring in her comings
And goings.
She carried pitchers of water
Hope the color of water.

She crossed borders
And everywhere
They detained her,
Accused her,
Examined her
As if she were an ill-omened bird.
Insatiable,
Determined,
Happy,
She crossed borders
Her body was a threshold
Where north and south
Were clear words
To wash the gaze
The heart
To polish cracks in the sand.

Ella cruzaba fronteras
Leía el cielo
Las palmas de sus pies
Celebraban
El ir y venir
El venir e ir
Imaginaba la libertad
Sus pies
Como piedras pulidas
Imaginaba que
Todos la nombraban
La reconocían
Que nadie la detenía
La devolvía
La revisaba
Ella era también
De este lugar.

She crossed borders
And read the sky
The soles of her feet
Celebrated
The comings and goings,
The goings and comings.
She imagined liberty
Her feet
Like polished stones
She imagined that
Everyone named her and
Recognized her
That no one detained her
Returned her
Searched her
She also belonged
Here.

A veces ella
Muy de a veces
Sale al jardín que
Ya no es jardín
Tan sólo el vasto silencio
De lo que no florece
Las sombras de la muerte
Que polulan
Pero sale al jardín
Intenta recordarse el nombre
De ciertas flores
Las amapolas rojas de su infancia.
A veces ella sale al jardín
Contempla la tierra
Rojiza con
Sus ojos empañados.
No hay a quien preguntar por las amapolas
Ni por los muertos que son tantos
A veces ella sale al jardín
Se toca el cuello
Desea cerciorarse si ella aun vive
Desea que alguien le coincida el don de una promesa.

Sometimes
Only sometimes she
Goes into the garden
Which is no longer a garden
Just the vast silence
Of that which doesn't blossom
The fluttering shadows
Of death.
But she goes into the garden
Trying to remember the names
Of certain flowers
The red poppies of her childhood.
Sometimes she goes out to the garden
To contemplate the
Reddish earth
With her blurry eyes.
There is no one to ask about the poppies
Or about the dead who are so many
Sometimes she goes out to the garden
And touches her neck
To make sure that she is still alive
Wishing that someone will give her the promise of hope.

Y ella se empina
Como una niña que aguarda
Regresos
Que espera promesas
Jardines nocturnos.

Y se empina cada noche
Como si sus ojos buscaran a
La hija extraviada en las dunas de Juarez.

A lo lejos tan sólo la noche densa
El silencio denso
La niebla negándole la mirada.

Y ella se empina
Como una niña que aguarda regresos.

She stands on tiptoe
Like a girl expecting
Returns
Waiting for promises
Nocturnal gardens.

Each night she stands on tiptoe
As if her eyes were searching for
The daughter missing in the Juárez dunes

In the distance only the dense night
The dense silence
The mist denying her vision.

And she stands on tiptoe
Like a girl expecting returns.

De María de Jesús González nada queda
Su madre cobija las prendas,
El vestido de percal perforado
Los cabellos despavoridos.
De María de Jesús tan sólo vestigios
Prendas distantes de lo que fue
Un vestido y una blusa.

Nothing remains of María de Jesús González
Her mother grasps the garments,
The dress of embroidered percale,
The terrified clumps of hair.
The only signs of María de Jesús
Distant garments of who she was
A dress and a blouse.

Les contaré de ellas.
Claro no son las señoritas glamorosas
Que viven en casas de cristal
La prensa ama recalcar la vida
De las desaparecidas con dinero
Con apellidos célebres
Con rostros de porcelana.

Las desaparecidas de Juárez son pobres
Sus vidas son oscuras, invisibles
Vienen de lugares extraños de la zona de Chihuahua
Algunas de Durango
Son delgadas y jóvenes
Sin caras de porcelana.
Nadie conoce sus apellidos:
Lozano, Pérez, Hernández
Nadie desea conmemorar sus muertes
Las señoritas extraviadas de Juárez
No tienen dinero
Mejor no hablar de ellas.

Cada noche alguna muerte
Y en el amanecer es una prisión de miedo
En las ciudades fronterizas es posible
No llegar nunca a ninguna frontera.

I will tell you about them.
To be sure, they aren't glamorous señoritas
Who live in glass houses
Or fall in love with celebrities.
The press loves to highlight the lives
of missing girls with money
With famous names
And porcelain faces.

The disappeared girls of Juárez are poor
Their lives are dark, invisible
They come from strange places in the State of Chihuahua
Some from Durango.
They are slender and young
And don't have porcelain faces.
No one knows their names:
Lozano, Pérez, Hernández
No one wants to commemorate their deaths
The missing señoritas of Juárez
Don't have money
It's better not to talk about them.

Each night someone dies
And daybreak is a prison of fear
In the cities along the border it's possible
To never make it to any border.

Me acerco a mi jardín nocturno
La quietud yace en la mirada
Avanzo en la desnudez
De una primera inocencia
La niebla me conduce
Hacia las flores que en la noche
Emiten fragancias extrañas
Presagios que embriagan
A lo lejos las luciérnagas
Iluminando travesías.

Me hundo en los paztizales
Alguien va conmigo
O es la sombra anónima?
Tal vez llevo el sueño de los
Jardines
El sol ha exhumado a la tierra
Para dejar el paso de la luna
Que brilla sobre las piedras.

Mis pasos, mis manos, la mirada
No acechan, se dejan de estar
La tierra es eterna en sus comienzos
Camino a tientas
Seguida por los espíritus tutelares
Por la pasión de una extranjera que
Es recibida en los jardines de la noche
Y es todo alrededor dicha, alquímia
Dorada sobre la oscuridad.

I approach my nocturnal garden
A stillness rests in my gaze
Advancing in the nakedness
Of an early innocence
The mist leads me
To the flowers that emit
Strange fragrances in the night
Omens that intoxicate
Distant fireflies
Illuminating crossings.

I sink into the pastures
Someone accompanies me
Or is it an anonymous shadow?
Maybe the gardens
Are in my dreams
The sun has left the earth
To make way for the moon
That shines on the rocks.

My steps, my hands, my gaze
Don't beseech, they let themselves be.
The earth is eternal in its beginnings
I grope in the dark
Followed by the tutelary spirits
By the passion of a foreigner who
Is received in the night gardens
And all around me is fortune,
A golden alchemy on the darkness.

No sé a quien encontraré
Pero me dejo llevar por la
Sinuosidad de las sombras que alarga mis caminos
El reflejo de mi cuerpo sobre las aguas imaginadas.

El jardín nocturno se revela
Y es nácar rocío envuelto en lágrimas
Exigue silencio
Grillos, lagartijas fosforescentes
Luciérnagas risueñas
Que traviesan me iluminan.

Todo es fluir de pasos
En la noche las cosas brotan
Y se revelan al que entiende sobre la
Magnitud
de las esperas
Sigilosa me deslizo
En la urdimbre de rosas purpúreas
Esto es el paraíso
Un relámpago, un eco
La noche sobre el verano
El verano, la noche
Costas.

I don't know who I will find
But I let myself be taken by the
Winding shadows that lengthen my journey
The reflection of my body on imagined waters.

The nocturnal garden reveals itself
It is dewdrop mother-of-pearl rolled up in tears
It demands silence
Crickets, phosphorescent lizards and
Cheerful fireflies
Illuminate me as they cross.

Everything is a flow of steps
In the night things sprout
And reveal themselves to those who understand
The magnitude
of patience.
Silently I slip
Into the tangle of purple roses
This is paradise
A flash of lightning, an echo
Night falling on summer
Summer falling on night
Shores.

Y es ese sentir
Como parpadeo
Asombro
Deslizarse por la piel
Intuir un día opalino
El aire, crisálidas de fragancias
Fragmentos de luz
Cruzando los bosques.

Y es ese placer de
Saberse viva
Habitada por el agua
Enhebrada a los precipicios
Al pequeño río que fluye y cesa
Con su acostumbrada quietud.

La vida se despliega
En su presencia mágica
Sin querer es plena
Y en su poder
La habitamos.

Todo es sutil y magnífico
Mis manos que parecen mirarse las
Unas a las otras
Onduladas como en la dirección del agua
En la luz que como el agua se vacía, se regenera
Es estrella
Firmamento.

Y aquí entre estos bosques donde yo escribo
Alguien susurra a mi oído que
Valía la pena esta vida.

It is that feeling
Like a flickering
Astonishment
To slide along the skin
To sense an opaline day
The air, a chrysalis of fragrances
Fragments of light
Crossing forests.

And it is that pleasure of
Knowing oneself alive
Inhabited by water
Threaded to the chasms
To the little river that ebbs and flows
With its accustomed stillness.

Life revealing itself
In its magical presence
Fortuitously, it is full
And with its power
We inhabit it.

All is subtle and magnificent
My hands seem to gaze
At one another
Waving in the direction of the water
In the light which like the water empties and regenerates
It is a star,
Firmament.

And here among the trees where I write
Someone whispers in my ear that
Life is worth living.

Tan sólo la muerte
Como una caricia
Bienvenida entre la mudez
Y el letargo
Tan sólo la muerte
Guardiana,
Angel de reposo
Tan sólo la muerte:
Mensajera del alivio
Repositora de ese cuerpo que no clama
Que no gime
Que no es
Tan sólo la muerte
Reconoce el espanto
Se la envuelve toda
Apacigua su cuerpo desbandado
Se la lleva al jardín
Nocturno
Lejos del desierto.

Only death
Like a caress
Welcome among muteness
And lethargy
Only death
Guardian
Angel of repose
Only death:
Messenger of relief
Repository of that body that doesn't cry out
That doesn't moan
That no longer is
Only death
Recognizes terror
And surrounds everything
Soothing her scattered remains,
It brings her to a
Nocturnal garden
Far from the desert.

He ido con tu nombre
Por los campos
He entrado a ciudades deshabitadas
Donde los pájaros mueren en la noche
Te he buscado
Entre los mudos
Las mujeres que sólo miran perdidas
Hacia el horizonte
He viajado contigo y tu nombre
En busca de tu luz
He repetido tu nombre hasta
Ser un sueño perdido en las planicies
Y nadie responde nadie reconoce
Nadie indaga
Tan sólo tu nombre
En mis labios secos
Tan sólo tu nombre que te recuerda
Palpear esencias, despertarse sola
Con tu nombre como una ceniza que nubla la luz.

I have wandered the countryside
With your name
I have entered uninhabited cities
Where birds die at night
I have looked for you
Among the silent ones
Women who only gaze toward the horizon
At their losses.
I have wandered with you and your name
In search of your light
And have repeated it until
It has become a dream on the wasteland
And no one responds, no one recognizes
No one inquires
Only your name
On my dry lips
Only your name that remembers you
To touch absences, to awaken alone
With your name like ashes that cloud the light.

Fronteras

Ella soñaba con las fronteras
Traspasarlas, dejarlas entrar a ellas
Ser otra y no ser otra
Cruzar viajar inventarse otro paisaje
Su madre le decía:
Ten cuidado con las fronteras
Las mujeres no deben salir de casa
Que las palabras no le alcanzarían para salvarse
que las mujeres pobres no saben salvarse por medio
De las palabras.

Ella sueña con las fronteras
Y una noche donde la luna es una mujer redonda y calmada
Las cruza
Sus pies conocen el desierto de la noche
Los sonidos del vacío
Los sonidos de la ausencia
Las horas de la muerte.

Llueve
Y tan sólo la muerte la aguarda
Como los sueños que le presagiaban las curanderas
Las abuelas de Chihuahua.

Borders

She was dreaming about borders
To cross them and gain permission to enter them
To be another and not to be another
To cross, to travel and to invent another landscape.
Her mother would tell her:
Be careful at the border
Women should not leave home
Words would not be sufficient to save oneself
Poor women don't know how to save themselves
Through words.

She dreams about borders
And on a night when the moon is full and calm like a woman
She crosses them
Her feet know the night desert
The sounds of emptiness
The sounds of absence
The hours of death.

It rains
And only death awaits her
Like in the dreams foretold to her by the wise women
The grandmothers of Chihuahua.

Ella sueña con las fronteras
Un cuchillo la atraviesa en dos
El norte y el sur
El cuerpo de una mujer yace
En medio de la noche
En medio del día
En medio de la luz
En la frontera nadie la encuentra
El desierto petrifica su memoria
El viento borra los sonidos
Todo es oscuridad sin sol.

Ella ha cruzado fronteras
No regresa a casa
Su madre vaga llorando
La busca para no encontrarla.

Ella cruza fronteras
Vigilia y sueño
Cenizas y hogueras.

She dreams about borders
A knife parts her in two
North and South
The body of a woman lies
In the middle of the night
In the middle of the day
In the middle of the light
On the border no one finds her
The desert petrifies her memory
The wind erases sounds
Everything is a darkness without sunlight.

She has crossed borders
And doesn't return home
Her mother wanders about crying
And looks for but does not find her.

She crosses borders
Wakefulness and dream
Ashes and bonfires.

La memoria es el único testigo que
Recuerda a las mujeres de Juárez
Ahora estatuas
Ahora huesos derramados
Cabezas y orejitas.

Ahí se han quedado las mujeres de Juárez que
Han dejado sus alientos y sus vidas
Sus pasos sobre las arenas
Sus gemidos sobre mis manos que esculpen
Sus nombres en estas palabras
Que son rezo plegaria.

Memory is the only witness that
Remembers the women of Juárez
Now statues,
Scattered bones,
Heads and little ears.

There lie the remains of the women of Juárez
Who have left behind their spirits and lives
Their steps on the sand
Their moans on my hands that engrave
Their names in these words
That are a prayer, a supplication.

A veces las imagino
Exquisitas
Vestidas en la plenitud de
Las cosas ilusionadas.

Llegan a América
En esta tierra las aguarda la
Fortuna
Un dólar o dos al día.
En esta tierra
Las aguarda sólo
La muerte.

Sometimes I imagine them
Exquisite
Dressed in the fullness of
Airy hopes.

They come to America
To this land where
Fortune awaits them.
A dollar or two a day.
To this land
Where only death
Awaits them.

Aquella noche
Se lo dijeron:
La niña se había extraviado
La madre como una estatua
En el jardín de los muertos.

Aquella noche, la madre
Yacía inmóvil.
Supo que para los pobres no había justicia.
Frente al sopor del aire
Llegó la lluvia, le lavó el corazón,
Comenzó a danzar.
Tenía hambre
Tenía miedo
Su hija era ahora el número 278.

Aquella noche
Se sintió huérfana de hija
La vida le huía
La muerte danzaba alrededor
Con sus sombras
Con sus delantales plasmados
De pájaros muertos.

Aquella noche
Danzó para no dormir.

That night
They told her
The girl was missing.
The mother looked like a statue
In the garden of the dead.

That night, the mother
Rested motionless
She knew there was no justice for the poor.
Amid the stifling air
The rain came and washed her heart
She began to dance
She was hungry
And feared that
Her daughter was now number 278.

That night
She felt daughterless
Life eluded her
Death danced around
With its shadows and
Aprons made of
Dead birds.

That night
She danced so as not to sleep.

Atrévete
A una plegaria
Para las mujeres muertas
En ciudad Juárez
En las orillas de los ríos
En los estadios de Santiago de Chile
En aquella montaña cerca
del Mazote, en El Salvador
Cuando se las llevaron a ellas
A las niñas diminutas como sus
Muñecas de trapo.

Una plegaria para las mujeres vendadas
Que se les negó el derecho al don y a la palabra.
Una plegaria
Para no decir lo que no se dice,
Para rezar como se debe
Para cuestionar al cuerpo de los
Sacerdotes ungüentando el cuerpo
De las niñas
En el nombre de Dios.

Y en el nombre de Dios
Pongo en tela de juicio a sacerdotes
Y a los dueños de compañías
Porque las escondieron en los closets
Porque las obligaron a ser una sombra vigilada
En el nombre de Dios

Una plegaria
Una estrella
Una flor
Para las mujeres de Juárez
Para todas nosotras,
Para ellas.

Dare
To offer a supplication
For the dead women
of Ciudad Juárez
On the banks of the rivers
In the stadiums of Santiago de Chile
On that mountain near
El Mozote in El Salvador
Where they took them away
Young girls as petite as their
Rag dolls.

A prayer for the blindfolded women
Who were denied the right of free speech
A supplication
To speak the unspoken
To pray as one should
To question priests
Anointing the bodies
Of girls
In the name of God.

And in the name of God
I pass judgment on the priests
And heads of companies
Because they hid them in closets
And forced them to be supervised shadows
In the name of God.

A supplication
A star
A flower
For all the women of Juárez
For all of us
For them.

Van creciendo entre las planicies
Es imposible distinguir sus rostros
Tan sólo los rebozos que no
Ocultan la mirada.

Caminan ligeras
Como si danzaran
Y en esa danza
Gimen
Murmuran
Cantan.

Las he visto antes
En la antesala de mis sueños
En la despiadada Plaza de Mayo
En las murallas de Dubrovnik
Y todas ellas
Tienen el rostro turbio
La mirada piadosa.

They continue growing amid the wastelands
It's impossible to distinguish their faces
Only the shawls that don't
Hide the gaze.

They walk softly
As if they were dancing
And in that dance
They moan
Murmur
And sing.

I have seen them before
In the antechamber of my dreams
In the heartless Plaza de Mayo
On the walls of Dubrovnik
And they all
Have anxious
Pious gazes.

La justicia
Ante la muerte
Elegía a sus almas
Prefería a las muchachas rubias
Y blancas
Aquéllas de los suburbios
Y de padres obedientes en el orden
De los deberes
Padres de ocupaciones obsesivas
Amadores de todo tipo de posesiones
Inclinados a sólo palpar al mundo
A través de las imágenes.

Y la justicia
Protegía a la niña millonaria
Vestida de mujer
O a la religiosa de Iowa
O a las mujeres niñas que tenían
Historias de amor con políticos.

Siempre cautelosa la justicia con elecciones
Aludiendo a las etnias, al color de la piel.

Y los habitantes de América
Miran con deleite extasiados
Algunos son muy hábiles en el arte de llorar.

Before death
Justice
Chose its souls
It preferred blond girls
And white ones
Those from the suburbs
With obedient parents
In the order of duties.
Parents with obsessive occupations
Fond of all types of possessions
Inclined to only touch the world
Through images.

And Justice
Protected the millionaire girl
Dressed as a woman
Or the nun from Iowa
Or the young women who had
Love affairs with politicians.

Always cautious with its choices,
Justice heeded ethnicities and skin color.

And the residents of America
Gaze enraptured with delight
Some are very skillful in the art of crying.

En cambio
En aquella ciudad fronteriza
Con olor a muerte a desagües
Putrefactos con voces de mejicanos
Pululando entre el sopor de un calor de bestias.
La justicia se olvida de las muertes de Juárez
La policía bosteza
Unos dicen que andaban vestidas con ropas
Cortas demasiado cortas
Provocando a los asesinos que despúes
De todo eran hombres buenos.

La muerte llega a Juárez
Vestida de pobre
No usa tacos glamorosos
Ni mantones de manila.

Es terca
Sabe que nadie notará sus idas y venidas
Tan sólo las madres
Que creen que el alma regresa
Pero a Juárez nadie regresa.

La justicia sólo se ocupa de las niñas blancas
En las casas como fortalezas!

However
In that border town
With smells of death and sewers
Putrefied with the voices of Mexicans
Swarming amid the stupor of a bestial heat,
Justice forgets about the dead women of Juárez.
The police yawn
Some say they walked around wearing dresses
Much too short
Provoking the murderers who
After all, were good men.

Death comes to Juárez
Dressed as a poor girl
It doesn't wear elegant clothing
Or embroidered shawls.

It is stubborn
And knows that no one will notice its comings and goings
Only the mothers
Who believe that the soul returns
But no one returns to Juárez.

Justice only worries about the white girls
In fortress homes!

Lluvia

Ella siente la lluvia
Sobre el desierto
Como entonces
Unta sus manos en la
tierra sonámbula
Como entonces
Aguarda
Y entre la vastedad de la
Noche alguien
La nombra.

Rain

She feels the rain
On the desert.
As in another time
She rubs her hands in the
Somnolent earth.
As in another time
She awaits
And amid the vastness of the
Night someone
Names her.

Asombro

Pidió un deseo
Que se le conceda el don del
Asombro que el velo de la tristeza
Que cada noche empaña ese mirar
Se deslice del rostro
Que el santo padre le conceda
El don del asombro.

Wonder

She asked for one wish
That she be granted the gift of
Wonder and that the
Veil of sadness that dims her face
Each night, be lifted
That the Holy Father
Grant her the gift of wonder.

Noticieros

El noticiero de Ciudad Juárez
Anuncia otra muerte
Parece que es la misma mujer dice el niño
Todas las mujeres ésas son iguales responde el padre
La madre desgrana alimentos
Se reconoce en esas mujeres
El noticiero sigue
Anuncian los ganadores del torneo de fútbol
El niño pregunta a su mamá que por qué
Siempre matan a la misma mujer
La madre tiene una voz de extranjera
Una voz de niña
Y se hace un pozo de silencio
En su boca triste.

News Reports

The news report of Ciudad Juárez
Announces another death
The child says that it looks like the same woman
All of those women are the same, the father replies
The mother prepares the food
She sees herself in those women
The news report continues
They announce the winners of the soccer tournament
The child asks his mother why
They always kill the same woman
The mother's voice is strange
Like that of a little girl
And a well of silence
Forms on her sad mouth.

Ella cruza fronteras
Con su jean y
Camisa blanca
Teme la partida
Las adivinanzas del pueblo
Le aseguran la felicidad.

La niña cruza fronteras
Teme a la marcha
A los extranjeros en los caminos.

La niña sueña con el Nogal
La higuera
La locura del Nopal
A lo lejos su madre la despide
Con ramas de hojas santas.

La niña viajera
Cruza la frontera
Y ya no se reconoce.
La obligan a ser otra
Modular otros gestos
Otras voces.
Y al regresar a casa
No se encuentra
Ella a nadie reconoce
Y nadie la reconoce.

She crosses the borders
With her jeans
And white shirt
She fears the departure
The fortune tellers of the town
Assure her of happiness.

The young girl crosses the borders
She fears
The strangers in the roads.

The young girl dreams about Nogal*
The fig tree
The madness of Nopal*
In the distance, her mother bids her farewell
With the branches of holy leaves.

The girl traveller
Crosses the border
And no longer recognizes herself.
They obligate her to be another
To modulate other gestures
Other voices.
And on the return home
She cannot find herself
She recognizes no one
And no one recognizes her.

*Nogal is the walnut tree; nopal is the prickly pear.

Fue
Éste
El vivir con la muerte
Sentir sus pasos entre las
Sombras
Sus zapatos huesudos.

A veces era ella la que
Desfilaba desnuda
Sobre las tardes anonadadas
Esperaba la cita perfecta
La hora pérfida o deseada
Para que la acompañaran
A sus recintos
Donde el enigma es el único presagio.

Tú poco a poco
Y con la lentitud de las sabias
Tu voz se desaloja del lenguaje.

Y yo tan sólo muy
A la distancia,
Imaginaba tu cabello de sedas clara
Tu voz que era un cascabel de historias.

La muerte emite su juicio
El veredicto que marca el origen,
Y aunque es tan conocida y presente
El día que ella llega, nos tornamos vulnerables
Miedosos.
La desconocemos
Y a tientas nos preguntamos
Por qué llegó tan inoportuna.

It was
This
Living with death
Feeling its movements amid the
Shadows
Its skeletal shoes.

Sometimes it was death who
Marched naked
Among the annihilated afternoons
Awaiting the perfect date
The perfidious or desired hour
So that they would accompany her
To her corners
Where the enigma is the only omen.

Little by little
And slowly like the wise women,
Your voice dislodges from language.

And only from
A distance,
Could I imagine your clear silk hair
Your voice that chimed with stories.

Death emits her judgment
The verdict that marks beginnings
And although present and well-known
The day she arrives, we become vulnerable,
Fearful
We don't recognize her
And gropingly we ask ourselves
Why she arrived in such an untimely way.

Preguntas en las sombras

Poco a poco nos acostumbramos
A convivir con ella
Todos los días regresas en el
Lenguaje que te nombra
A veces el sueño se apiada de nosotras
Y te apareces
Pero es en el silencio
Cuando más te reconozco.
Despojada de sollozos
De inútiles interrogantes
Llegas y
Dialogo con tu voz
Que es un espectro.
Me envuelves con tu chal que es una estrella
Y apaciguas las iras y los temores.

Poco a poco vivimos contigo y con la muerte
A la vida no regresarás
Pero esta memoria viva
Es también esa otra vida que
Regresa, que indaga,
Que camina con confianza entre las
Interrogantes de las sombras.

Questions in the Shadows

Little by little we adjust
To living with it
Every day you return in
The language that names you.
Sometimes sleep takes pity on us
And you appear.
But it is in silence
When I most recognize you.
Deprived of sobs
And useless questions
You arrive
And I converse with your
Spectral voice.
You cover me with your shawl of stars
And soothe my anger and fears.

Little by little we live with your death
You will not return to the living
But this live memory
Is also that other life that
Returns, that inquires,
That walks with confidence amid
The questions in the shadows.

Noviembre primero

Todos los primeros de noviembre
Ella recuerda a las niñas muertas
Las que no murieron ni de enfermedades
Ni vejeces
La que un día dejó de regresar a casa
No acudió a las llamadas
Tras las colinas
La que se negó a los desafíos del viento.

Elige las flores tiernas
las que apenas se abren
Como si aun temieran el lapso
antes de nacer
El abrirse toda en la intemperie.

Los demás en el cementerio
Conversan con sus muertos
Y comen sus comidas favoritas
Se siente una plácida compañía entre ellos
Los que no están y los que están
La convivencia es plácida
Y se perdonan todos los pecados.

La madre visita a la niña muerta
A pesar de que nada de ella
Ha encontrado
Nada de ella ha regresado.
Tan sólo quedan sus vestidos
Los zapatos de charol
Las páginas de un diario de vida
Esta vez siempre vacías
Como los espacios de una página en blanco
O una vida atravesada por los silencios.

November 1

Every November first
She remembers the dead girls
Those who didn't die from sickness
Or old age
The one who stopped coming home one day
Who didn't respond to the calls
Behind the hills
The girl who defied the howls of the wind.

She chooses the tender flowers
That barely open
As if they still feared
The instant before birth
Exposing themselves completely to the elements.

The others in the cemetery
Talk with their dead
And eat their favorite foods
They are all in good company
Those who are and are not present.
Being together is pleasant
All sins are forgiven.

The mother visits her dead daughter
Although her remains
Have not been found.
None of her has returned
Only her dresses remain
The patent leather shoes
The pages of an
Always empty diary
Like the spaces on a blank page
Or a life pierced by silence.

Los ruidos de la muerte

Nunca antes sentí
Los ruidos de la muerte
Una lechuza agonizando
En un cielo rojizo
Una mudez más allá
De todas las mudezas
El cielo vacío
La tierra ansiosa.

Death Rattles

Never before did I feel
Death rattles
An owl agonizing
In a red-stained sky
A muteness beyond
All silence
The empty sky
The anxious earth.

La tierra

Te preguntaba cómo era la tierra
Muy al fondo
Entre la angostura de la oscuridad
Y las aperturas de un cielo subterráneo.
Sonreías
Decías que los gusanos gobernaban la vida de
Los muertos
Que la tierra era huesuda y oscura pero
Para los que mueren con felicidad
Es tierna y dulce.

The Earth

I asked you what the earth was like
Deep inside
Amid the expanse of darkness
And the openings of a subterranean sky.
You smiled
Saying that worms governed the lives of
The dead
That the earth was dark and bony, but
That for those who die happy
It is sweet and tender.

El duelo

El duelo se hizo
Aprendizaje.
Se dejó llevar por la
Memoria infinita.
El duelo enseñó que para
La muerte no había consuelo
Ni palabras sabias
Ni el reposo de haber
Vivido con inocencia.

El duelo me enseñó
A palpar ausencias
A ver cosas entre otras cosas
Pensar que tal vez la muerte regresa
Por las noches como un buho que brinda
Noticias y extrañezas
O es una mariposa
Soberana y cobriza?

El duelo me enseñó a vivir el
Día y la noche
Sin pensar ni en orden ni en desórdenes
Dejar que el cuerpo, la soberanía del alma
Sigan sus pasos
Sus soledades perpétuas.

Fui aprendiendo a vivir
Con la muerte
A palpar tu vida en todos los vacíos
A nombrarte entre las sombras.

Sorrow

Grief became
An apprenticeship.
It allowed itself to be carried by
Infinite memory.
The pain revealed that for
Death there was no consolation
Nor wise words
Nor the peace that comes from
Having lived with innocence.

Grief taught me
To touch absences
To see things among other things
To think that perhaps death returns
In the night like an owl that offers
News and strange happenings
Or is it like a butterfly
Copper-toned and sovereign?

Grief taught me to live
Day and night
Without thinking about order and disorder
To let the body and the sovereignty of the soul
Follow their steps
Their perpetual solitude.

I continued learning to live
With death
To touch your life in the surrounding emptiness
To name you among the shadows.

De pronto
La lluvia en el desierto
Como una bendición solitaria
Como el camino truncado
De los muertos.

Cuando llueve
La madre piensa que
Es su hija
La que viene
La que obsequia aguas frescas
Para una tierra precaria
Y oscura.

Suddenly
Rain falls in the desert
Like a solitary blessing
A truncated path
Of the dead.

When it rains
The mother thinks that
It is her daughter
Who comes
To offer fresh water
To the dark
And precarious earth.

El dolor

I

El dolor se enraizó en el cabello
Palpó la nuca
Roció la boca de sequedades
De aquel paisaje donde yo jamás
Sabía posible habitarme
Deshabitada vivía junto al dolor
Como en un pozo oscuro
Sin lecho,
Sin tiempo,
Sin remanso.

II

Y el dolor se inclinó junto a mí
Sin premura
Me aligeró el cuerpo
Me enseñó a convivir con él
A sentirlo llegar como si fuera
El aire más dulce
La paz más soberana
Y así pude por fin vivir contigo
Sobrellevar la muerte
No anularla
No negarla
Pero vivirla
A tu lado
Sentir que no llegaré a encontrar
Tus pasos ni tu frente
Ni tus manos que ahora son
Mariposas traviesas.

Pain

I

Grief rooted itself in my hair
It touched the nape of my neck
It rubbed my parched mouth
In that landscape where I never
Believed it possible to live.
Uninhabited I lived next to the pain,
As in a dark
Bottomless
Timeless
Restless well.

II
Grief leaned toward me
Slowly
It lightened my body
It taught me to live with it
To feel it arrive as if it were
The sweetest air
The most sovereign peace.
And thus, I finally was able to live with you
To endure death
Not annul it
Or negate it
But live it
By your side
To feel that I will never find
Your footsteps or your face
Not even your hands that are now
Mischievous butterflies.

Entonces se mece
Como un río
Habla como un río
Ama como ese río que ahora
Es garganta seca
Lecho inquieto sin voz
Y es el río, la voz detrás
De otra voz.

La madre canta
La hija es el rehén que
Escucha
El río es un salto de vida
Una mirada de agua
Refugio
Emboscada
Memoria obstinada.

Y al regresar del río
Cuando la noche se hace áspera
Y la quietud desolada late
Como el reloj de todos los tiempos extraviados.
Ella
La madre
Lleva a su almohada
Piedrecillas del río
Que mecen su sueño
Que son piedras tutelares
Piedras que en la noche enmascarada
Le cuentan cosas de la niña
Perdida en el río.

She ebbs and flows
Like a river
She speaks like a river
And loves like that river that is now
A dry gorge
A restless bed without a voice
And it is the river, the voice behind
The other voice.

The mother sings
Her daughter is the hostage who
Listens
The river is a splash of life
A gaze of water
Refuge
Ambush
Obstinate memory.

Upon returning from the river
When the night becomes harsh
And the desolate stillness throbs
Like a clock of lost times
She
The mother
Brings river stones to
Her pillow
That rock her dreams
Like protective amulets
Stones that in the concealed night
Tell her things about the
Lost girl in the river.

Regresas ligera de equipaje
Donde nadie te reconoce
Y los que quedan
Sólo conversan con los muertos.
Regresas a un país ya perdido
A un sinuoso horizonte doblegado por
la historia.

La casa de tu madre
A nadie vigila
Nadie se preocupa por tus
Andanzas
Nadie adivina la ilusión de tus
Regresos.

Has vuelto al país de los muertos
A la soberanía de la ausencia
Las mesas vacías
Las sillas mancas
Las fiestas entre los que sólo
Rememoran
Para que ellos tampoco se olviden.

You return, light of provisions
Where no one recognizes you
And those who remain
Only speak with the dead.
You return to a country already lost
To a sinuous horizon subdued
By history.

Your mother's house
Doesn't harbor anyone.
No one worries about your
Comings and goings.
No one divines the illusion of your
Returns.

You have come back to the country of the dead
To the sovereignty of absence
Empty tables
Maimed chairs
Parties among those who only
Remember
So that they will never forget.

Y sin embargo regresas
Hallas consuelo en que alguien
A lo lejos te haga señas
Y no sabes ni preguntas
Si es él del reino de los vivos
O de los muertos.

Has aprendido a rendir espacios a los
Silencios
A vivir entre una marejada de dudas
La ambigüedad te cobija
Le sonríes
Regresas.

And nonetheless you return
Finding comfort in the hope that someone
Will make signs to you from afar
And you don´t know or ask
If he is from the kingdom of the living
Or of the dead.

You have learned to yield space to
The silences
To live amid a ground swell of doubt
Ambiguity protects you
Smiling at it
You return.

Y el mar fue un
Privilegio del reconocimiento
Aprendizaje de la mirada
Sobre un movimiento que exige la hipnótica
Paciencia
El privilegio de la fe que
Es cadencia
Erupción de secretos.

Y así junto al mar me dejé llevar en
La plenitud inexacta de
Las horas
Guiándome por el ritmo, el sonido
Lo que la ola regresa
Lo que la ola lleva

And the sea was a
Privilege of recognition
Apprenticeship of the gaze
Over a movement that demands hypnotic
Patience
The privilege of faith that
Is a cadence
An eruption of secrets.

And thus, next to the sea I let
Myself be carried by the imprecise plenitude of
The hours
Guiding myself by the rhythm, the sound
Of what the wave returns
And takes away.

Y el aprendizaje fue amar
La lentitud
Dejar el quehacer
Dejar sólo el murmullo
Una brisa
La arena insinuando un poema.

The learning was in loving
The slowness
Leaving behind tasks
Leaving only the murmur
A breeze
The sand insinuating a poem.

La arena

Digna en su impermanencia
La arena enseña
La presencia solitaria de la marcha
El poema escrito sobre ella
La debilidad que borra la fatua
Presencia de las palabras

La arena es
El paso de un angel
Extraviado
Que no exige permanencias.

Sand

Deserving in its impermanence
The sand demonstrates
The solitary presence of the passage of time
The poem written on it
The weakness that erases the fatuous
Presence of words.

The sand is
A drifting
Lost angel
That does not demand permanences.

Aprendizaje

El aprendizaje yace
En lo invisible
Saber lo que la oscuridad
Enciende
Lo que la flor confirma
Lo que la paz
Señala.

El aprendizaje es
un lenguaje que desroba.

Silencio

Entonces llegó el silencio
No trajo ni ofrendas ni temores
Tan sólo otro lenguaje
Certero húmedo
Cavidad de sonidos.

Learning

Learning resides
In the invisible
Knowing what the darkness
Illuminates
What the flower confirms
What peace
Identifies.

Learning is
A language that disrobes.

Silence

Then the silence came
Not bringing offerings or fears
Only another language
A humid sceptre
A cavity of sounds.

Amapolas

Me detuve entre las amapolas
Las pensé en California
En las costas de Cataluña
Parecían ser un collar indomable
De pétalos y rastros
No pertenecían a ninguna nación
Más que a la tierra.

Tan sólo la memoria

Era tan sólo
La memoria,
Fugaz travesía
Como una noche sin espejo,
Como quien busca la incertidumbre
De la fe.

Poppies

I paused among the poppies
I thought about them in California
And on the Catalan coast
They seemed like a wild necklace
Of petals and signs
That didn't belong to any nation
Only the earth.

Only Memory

It was only
Memory,
Fleeting voyage
Like a mirrorless night
Like someone searching for the uncertainty
Of faith.

Tal vez no deberíamos
Haber dejado
La patria
Ni el pueblo, ni la calle.
Tal vez deberíamos haber
Conocido más a los amigos
Buscar los huertos
La paz de los limoneros.
Tan sólo deberíamos habernos
Quedado en el café de la esquina,
O en el barrio mirando un partido
De fútbol con los vecinos.
Tal vez la nostalgia sería
Algo que les pasaba a otros.
Tal vez nunca nos deberíamos haber ido
De casa
Ni hecho el amor en idiomas
Prestados
Tal vez . . .

Perhaps we should not
Have left
Our country
Our town or our street.
Perhaps we should have
Spent more time with our friends
And looked for orchards
The peace of the lemon groves.
If only we had stayed
At the corner coffee shop,
Or in the barrio looking at a soccer match
Together with the neighbors.
Perhaps nostalgia was something
That happened to others.
Perhaps we never should have
Left home
Or made love in
Borrowed languages
Perhaps . . .

Silencio

Y el paisaje fue silencio de noche larga
Donde no había ni origen ni vacío
Tan sólo la muerte seduciendo un lugar sin horas,
Tan sólo los latidos imaginarios de una mujer
A la orilla de la vida
Con una estrella de mar seco
Entre las manos.

Y su sueño se hizo
Una hebra perpetua
Estrella de agua
Tiempo sin tiempo.

No tuve más opción
Que defender con ternura
El color de mis sueños.

Silence

The landscape was a long, silent night
Where there was no beginning, no vacuum
Only death seducing a timeless place
Only the imaginary heartbeats of a woman
At the edge of life
With a dry star fish
Between her hands.

And her dream became
A perpetual thread
A strand of water
Timeless time.

I had no other option
But to defend with tenderness
The color of my dreams.

Ella elige
El verano
Para reconocer
Su piel
Grietas sobre sus brazos
Una intemperie desprevenida
Donde es imposible esconder
El rencor
O la ira de aquellas
Noches donde el
Invierno encierra
Su voz.

Ahora ella se deja reconocer
Junto al agua,
En las imágenes del agua,
Que alargan sus formas
Que diluyen sus dudas.

En el verano la brisa salina
La reconoce logrando
Detenerse en su cuerpo que ya
Se deja acompañar por el peso
De los años
Por las piernas raídas
Pero aún ella se siente
Ajena.
Amanece distinta
Cuando imagina arenas
Y recuerda desvanecidos
O recuerda objetos de la memoria que es
Un vacío
Una intemperie.

She chooses
Summer
To recognize
Her skin
The veins along her arms
A sudden storm
Where it is impossible to hide
Bitterness
Or the anger of those
Nights when
Winter locks up
Her voice.

Now she reveals herself
Next to the water
In the images of water
That elongate her form
That dilute her doubts.

In the summer the salty breeze
Recognizes her managing
To linger in a body that
Allows itself to be accompanied
By the weight of time
By the scraped legs.
But she still feels
Foreign.
At dawn she wakes a different being
When she imagines sand
And remembers vanishing objects to
Rescue them from a memory that is
Vacant
Unsheltered.

En el verano cerca del
Agua
En la plenitud de los bosques
Ella es también una estrella
Fugaz reposando sobre la noche
Clara
O una amapola que
Reposa en su
Vestido rojo
Incendiado de amores.

Es en el verano donde
Ella ilumina los sueños
Atrás deja las sombras
El jardín de invierno que es
Su mirada.
Y entiende del
Regocijo de la vida
Breve
De la intensidad soleada
De sus manos
De sentir el delirio del viento
Y nada más
Regocijo de la vida breve
Verano despoblado de futuro
Un día
Rojizo como la amapola
Que cae lentamente sobre sus pies.

In the summer near
The water
In the plenitude of the forest
She is also a shooting star
Resting on the
Clear night
Or a poppy that
Reclines in its
Red dress
Inflamed by love.

It is summer where
She illuminates her dreams
Leaving behind the shadows
The winter garden that is
Her gaze.
And she understands
The joy of a
Short life
The sunbathed intensity
Of her hands
Feeling the delirium of the wind
And nothing more.
The joy of a short life
A summer stripped of a future
A day
Red like the poppy
That slowly alights on her feet.

Larga y honda la noche
Del desierto
Todo y nada transcurre
Los pájaros meciéndose en el vacío
Del aire
El angel de la muerte
Los ahuyenta
Hoy como ayer
Otra mujer muere
En ciudad Juárez.

En ciudad Juárez las luces festivas
La música estridente
Las calles vestidas de rojo
Para ocultar la otra oscuridad
Del miedo
Del dolor clausurado
De los que mienten.

Long and deep is the
Desert night
Where everything and nothing happens
Birds rocking in the empty
Air
The Angel of Death
chases them away
Today like yesterday
Another woman dies
In Ciudad Juárez.

In Ciudad Juárez festive lights
Strident music
Streets dressed in red
To hide the other darkness
Of fear
Of cloistered pain
Of those who lie.

La niña de ciudad Juárez
Regresa a casa vestida de
Novia muerta.

La madre solloza en las colinas
Buscando ramas de tierra santa.

The young girl of Ciudad Juárez
Returns home dressed as a
Dead bride.

The mother wails amid the hills
Looking for pieces of holy earth.

—

Poems by
Guadalupe Morfin

Poema para el agua del desierto

¿Dé dónde, si no del desierto
esta agua limpísima
nobleza de la escasez
este incesante flujo de un manantial
que pocos adivinan?

¿A medida de qué estamos hechos
a imagen de quién?

¿No era ésta la tierra del abrigo
el refugio de los perseguidos
el último contacto con lo familiar
al lado sur del río, la entrada
a la blancura mítica de las arenas
mecidas sierra abajo por un viento
que nunca termina de peinar pedruscos?

¿No era de aquí el vigor
del último pecho erguido de la patria
el postrer filón de una dignidad
de laboriosa pobreza
empeñada en arrancar sombras de árbol
justo allí donde sólo crece
el silencio infinito de una estación sedienta?

¿Qué no pasaba por aquí un tren
de ida y vuelta
en cuyo chirriar se oía
el rumor del diálogo
entre los pueblos del norte y los del sur?

Poem Regarding Desert Water

From where else, but the desert
this pure water
nobility of what is frugal
this incessant flow from a spring
that few divine?

What are we made of
and in whose image?

Wasn't this the land of shelter
the refuge of the persecuted
the last contact with what is familiar
on the south side of the river, the entrance
to the mythical whiteness of sand
rocked to and fro at the foot of the mountain by a wind
that never stops combing rough stones?

Isn't it here where the last
act of our country's bravery was raised
the last lode of a dignity stemming
from arduous poverty
bent on pulling the tree's shadows
right there where all that grows
is the infinite silence of a parched season?

Didn't a round-trip train
pass through here
chattering along in what sounded like
the murmur of a dialogue
between towns of the north and south?

¿No era ése el río metálico
donde la luna rielaba su pasaje
de viaje y tolerancia?
¿No era acaso nuestro el río?

¿Y cuándo y por qué
comenzó a llenarse de sangre
la hora del crepúsculo
el suave balar de las ovejas
en espera del rito?

¿Qué conjunto de trampas fue preciso
poner a la femineidad
y qué señuelos
qué cuentas de cristal
cuántas promesas y cuentos de oropel
cuánta oferta de "se busca señorita"
"vacantes" "medios turnos"
cuánto engaño:
"transporte" "guardería" "salario"
"prestaciones" "becas" "alimentos"?

¿Y qué pasó con los niños, di,
quién les contó los cuentos
y qué mano les puso un manto encima
para el frío
y por qué este silencio de los hombres
este hacerse a un lado este rencor
este cáncer de callar dolores
y la grieta en la piel por sofocar el grito y el reclamo?

Wasn't that the metallic river
where the moon cast its impression
of journeys and tolerance?
Was that not our river?

When and why did the twilight
begin to fill with blood
the soft bleating of the sheep
awaiting the ritual?

What set of traps was it necessary
to place on femininity
and what lures
what crystal beads
how many hollow promises and stories
how many requests for "Young Girl Wanted"
"Vacancy" "Part Time"
how many deceptions:
"Transportation," "Day Care," "Salary,"
"Loans," "Scholarships," "Food"?

And what happened to the children, tell me
who told them stories
and what hand covered them with a blanket for the cold
and why this silence from the men
this putting anger aside
this cancer of silencing grief
and the crack in the skin from stifling the protest and cry?

Se están llevando a tus hijas
¿No dices nada?
¿Eso te han enseñado?
Y quién te dijo que los hombres no lloran
¿quién?

Porque, mira, esta agua limpísima
que da alivio a mi cuerpo
no viene del desierto
ni de ocultos manantiales
es el llanto de todos los que lloran
en esta larga noche
mientras otros afilan su impotencia
y salen, rabiosos y ebrios,
tras su cacería de ovejas.

 Aquí no se oye ladrar a los perros
aquí, entre el lote baldío y el deshuesadero
sólo gime el viento
y alguien carga y viste
una a una a las niñas
y luego aparecen y nos dicen
que nada será en vano
nada
ninguna lágrima
ninguna.

They are taking your daughters
You have nothing to say?
Is this what they've taught you?
And who told you that men don't cry?
Who?

Because, look here
this pure water
that relieves my body
does not come from the desert
or from hidden springs
It is from the tears of all who cry
through this long night
while others sharpen their impotence
and leave, rabid and drunk,
after hunting for sheep.

There is no sound of barking dogs
here, between the vacant lot and the heap of bones
the wind only moans
and someone carries and dresses
the young girls, one by one
and then they appear and tell us
that nothing will be in vain
nothing
not one tear
not one.

Tierra de ceniza

Y aquí en las arenas, dime, ¿se puede amar?

¿No es acaso espiritual esta nada
esta tierra que se mesa los cabellos
como mujer a la que han robado las hijas
cubierta de cenizas
en su perpetua estación de duelo?

¿No es aquí cuaresma
incluso en el adviento?
¿Despedida al llegar
y en el ir llegando arraigo?

¿No es aquí donde todo obliga
a mirar a lo alto
                        en busca de color
o hacia el centro mismo de todo
en persecución ahogada
de una forma antigua de respirar?

No me digas que no has amado sus inviernos
las coronas nevadas de sus más altas piedras
su disimulo de todo lo que florece
no se vaya a despertar más avaricia yanqui
no salgan más demonios a buscar a las niñas
y todo sea otra vez rojo
como una cascada del corazón abierto
que salpica los campos de golf
las avenidas
los malls de la ciudad vecina
las conciencias
los zapatos de quienes nunca visitaron
estas tierras de nadie

Land of Ashes

Here in the sand, tell me: Can one love?

Isn't this nothingness almost spiritual
this land that tears at its hair
like a woman whose daughters have been stolen
covered in ashes
in its perpetual state of mourning?

Isn't it Lent here,
even during Advent?
A farewell upon arrival
a rootedness in departure?

Isn't it here where all are compelled
to gaze upward
                in search of color
or toward the very center
in a stifled pursuit
of an ancient form of breathing?

Don't tell me that you haven't loved winters here
the snowy peaks of the highest rocks
the pretense of all that blossoms.
Let there be no more awakening of *yanqui* greed
or demons searching for girls
so that all is once again red
like a waterfall bursting from an open heart
that splashes over golf courses
avenues
the malls of the neighboring city
the conscience
and shoes of those who never visited
these no man's lands

esta expresión de horror urbano
donde una llanta de automóvil
es un escalón a la puerta de casa
un perro el mejor policía
un montón de polvo el escenario
de juego para los niños
cuyas canicas se resisten a rodar.

No me digas que no
si estás amando descifrar sus claves
despertar con sus silencios
acogerte
a la luz matinal de sus cerros vecinos.

Y el crepúsculo, por Dios,

¿no es acaso un Cristo
allá en el horizonte
lo que se ha puesto a caminar
como un fantasma más entre los vivos?

¿No oyes cómo se jala los cabellos
esta tierra de arenas y pedruscos
este vertedero echado a gemir
por las niñas perdidas
las niñas nuestras
las niñas halladas con las pupilas fijas
en otro más allá
                    otra justicia
                    otro ser mujer distinto
mientras los garfios se hunden en la carne
y tú y yo preguntándonos
si es posible amar
cuando es sólo el amor lo que nos tiene aquí
a mí temblando

this expression of urban horror
where an automobile tire
is a step at the door of a house
a dog, the best policeman
a heap of dust the scene
of a children's game
in which the marbles refuse to roll.

Don't tell me that you haven't. . .
if you love deciphering her secrets
waking among her silences
and taking refuge
in the morning light of the neighboring hills.

And the twilight, as God is my witness,

Might it not be a Christ
there in the horizon
who has begun to walk
like one more ghost among the living?

Can't you hear how this earth pulls its hair
like a grieving mother
this dumping ground of sand and pebbles
has begun to moan
for the lost girls
our own girls
found with their eyes staring
at another afterlife
        another form of justice
        another way of being?
while the hooks sink into the flesh
and you and I ask ourselves
if it is possible to love
when love is all that keeps us here

contigo lejos
y los hijos que vendrán a hacernos compañía
justo para poner el árbol de las estrellas
y seguir cantando
cada estación, amado,
cada paso
esta noble ceniza
de un adviento que no acaba de llegar.

keeps me trembling
with you far away
and the children who will accompany us
to decorate the tree with stars
and continue singing
each season, beloved,
each step
this noble ash
of an Advent that does not arrive.

About the Contributors

MARJORIE AGOSÍN is a native of Chile and professor of Latin American literature at Wellesley College. She is the author of more than twenty published volumes of prose and poetry and has been the recipient of awards that have recognized her tireless efforts in the realm of human rights and her dedication to the world of the literary imagination. She has also been a visiting artist and scholar at several universities in the U.S. and abroad, including the University of Los Andes, the University of Georgia, and Columbia University. Her most distiguished honors include the United Nations Leadership Award on Human Rights, the Henrietta Zold Award and the Letras de Oro Prize. Among her most recent books are: A *Map of Hope: Women's Writing on Human Rights, To Mend the World: Women Respond to 9/11* and *The Angel of Memory.*

CELESTE KOSTOPULOS-COOPERMAN is a professor of humanities and modern languages and director of the Latin American and Caribbean studies program at Suffolk University, Boston, Massachusetts. Her special areas of concentration are in modern and contemporary Latin American prose and poetry, women's literature, political and human rights narratives and translation theory and practice. Her translations have appeared in such distinguished journals as *Agni, The American Voice, Harpers, Human Rights Quarterly* and the *Michigan Quarterly Review.* Recipient of the Outstanding Translation Award from the American Literary Translators Assosciation for *Circles of Madness* (New York: White Pine Press, 1992), her most recent publication, also with White Pine Press, is *At the Threshold of Memory: Selected and New Poems* by Marjorie Agosín, 2003.

GUADALUPE MORFIN was appointed by President Vicente Fox in October of 2003 as the special federal commissioner on violence against women in Ciudad Juarez, Mexico. She has a broad mandate to coordinate federal programs to prevent and also investigate violence against women. She also is responsible for coordinating these efforts with state and municipal policies. In her report, *Informe de gestion (noviembre 2003-abril 2004)* she provides an analysis of the root causes of violence against women in Juarez and is strongly critical of state and federal officials for failing to protect the families of the victims and their advocates. In her current position she continues to search for truth and justice and to look for ways to identify and eliminate the origins of the violence and to restore dignity to the families of the disappeared and murdered young women.

LYDIA MARTIN is an associate professor of art at the New England School of Art and Design at Suffolk University, Boston, Massachusetts, where she teaches drawing, painting and perspective within the Foundation Program. A contemporary realist painter, her applied techniques are primarily classical, although she turns habitually to John Singer Sargent for understanding of color and to Claudio Bravo for matters of expression and composition. She has painted numerous commissioned works and has received top awards for oil painting from the Catherine Lorilard Wolfe Arts Club in New York City, Harvard University's Arnold Arboretum and the St. Louis Artisits' Guild. Her painting, "The Border," adorns the cover of this book.